The Mind Games Women Play On Men

By Tonya Love

I0426465

Table of Contents

Chapter One – Introduction

Psychobabble is not my thing, and I aim to break this topic down to you once and for all! For centuries men have been trying to understand women and their manipulative behaviors. They want to know what it is that makes the sweetest, most loving woman turn into a seemingly raging lunatic. I'm assuming since you bought this book, you have gone out with women like this, and you are seeking answers. There are many topics that I would like to touch upon, all the while filling the pages with things that I am sure you will remember, and stories that all men can relate to.

Now a days most people have a computer, and internet access. I'm sure if you want to, you can locate a few answers on Google, but through my own research I have yet to find one single resource dedicated to addressing your most common questions immediately and clearly. I'm not going to claim that I know everything, or that this is the only book you will ever need to figure out women, but I am going to say that it *WILL* shed some light on those dark twisty places that are covered by beautiful faces. There are plenty of good women out there who do not "try" to manipulate others, and it's totally unfair to say that all women are the same. That would be like saying that all babies look the same when they are born, or that all kids have the same personalities. Obviously this is false.

Some have dark hair, some have light

hair. Some are funny, some are trouble makers. The same with women, each has their own unique qualities and flaws. No one is perfect. Just for the sake of this book though, I will go ahead and use the word, "game" to indicate the manipulative types of behavior that one can encounter while being in the company of women. They don't necessarily have to be your girl friend either – this goes for your mom, sister, aunt, and grandmother too. If you tangle yourself up with the wrong kind of woman, you could seriously end up with a massively huge heartache. I have high hopes that I can prevent some of that for you, and you can counteract manipulative behaviors in order to form happy, lasting relationships in your life.

Let's first start by understanding any

terms that you might want to know before getting on with the rest of this book. I'm not saying you're not smart, but some of us may not think about the topic all too often, and it might help to better understand where I am coming from.

Manipulation – the dictionary says that this word means to control or play upon by artful, unfair, or insidious means especially to one's own advantage. Another definition is to change by artful or unfair means so as to serve one's purpose. Manipulation is something that we have all used at least one time or another in our lives. No sense saying any different. I am sure your own manipulation started as a baby crying out to your mom in a way that made her feel bad for you so that she would pick you up and hold you. Manipulation can be as innocent as adding numbers in your head instead of writing your explanation on paper. Or it can be as dangerous as a blatant attempt to manipulate the public to carry guns for their own protection when they are not allowed by law.

Another term that you might see me use a lot is *narcissism* or *narcissistic* – which the dictionary defines as egocentric, or in love with one's own self or body. This might seem a little bit of a silly definition, but I like to say that narcissistic people are in love with their own reflection in the mirror! Everything that they do is for themselves, and not for the benefit of anyone else. A certain amount of narcissism is healthy. One should care about themselves and value their own needs. I'm just talking about the ones who go above and beyond this need, and hurt others in the process. Then it becomes a disorder. Both men and women can fall under this category. But for the sake of this book, I will mainly talk about women. To my own surprise, there are plenty of these types of personalities roaming the world today. I'd recommend getting a good book about this type of disorder and reading up on it. It too may save you a lot of troubles and painful good byes in your future.

Again, I will say that the purpose of this book is not to vilify women or those with narcissistic personalities. My purpose is to shed light on these destructive dynamics that cause unhealthy relationships. Knowledge is power, and this will help you equip yourself for the unexpected, and help you know when to walk away if necessary. No one wants to be strapped down to someone who makes you unhappy and plays mind games with you all day. Life is too short.

I have chosen 23 of the most common games that women play with men in order to keep control over the relationship. So with that said, read on and tuck these tips into your memory bank for a later time when it's useful and needed. I doubt there will be anyone who reads this book who can not relate to the topics discussed in these pages.

Chapter Two

The Praising Game

So you've found yourself the perfect woman, and the two of you have really hit it off. In fact, you get along so well that you doubt you will ever get in a fight, right? All of a sudden, she can't stop praising you and stroking your ego. Sure, it feels pretty darn good, but why on earth is she being *so nice?*

This morning instead of rolling out of bed to your normal cup of black coffee, and bowl of cereal, you find her in the kitchen cooking you breakfast. The house is full of all the lovely aromas all mixed together, totally making your mouth water. She has spent almost every night with you for the past two weeks, and never once cooked for you. This is where you need to put your sensibility intact, and ask yourself, "What's going on?" If you don't you will be totally caught off guard tonight when she asks you that special favor and you feel obligated to say, "yes" to her.

You can bet your bottom dollar that this change is totally with a reason in mind.
Of course women like to cook for their man sometimes, but when she starts becoming *overly nice to you*, there is usually something more she wants from you. You will find her praising you for taking out the trash, praising you for how cute you sound when you laugh, or how manly you are when you flex your arm muscles. Her attentions will be totally fixed on you and making you feel like the most irresistible man on earth. This is all done in the hopes that she can get

one up on you, and get you to pay her back the favor later.

Now I'm not saying that her praises don't feel good, or aren't entertaining to you. I'm just trying to prepare you for what might come next. She is clever and knows what she is doing, and it's only fair that you know too! So the next time you pull into the driveway after a long day at work, and she meets you at the front door telling you what a great provider you are – be warned that she is probably going to ask you for something. It might not be today, but she is buttering you up for whatever it is in the following days. In all honesty, it may not be a big deal at all to you. But the whole idea is to be able to read your partners actions, and turn them into something more positive. Getting along, sure beats fighting all the time, right? It might also be a good idea to play along with her a little bit. The warm welcome home felt pretty darn good – didn't it?

The Crying Game

You're a man, and you've been socially conditioned since you were a child to be rough and tough, allowing no one to see you cry. I bet if you think back, the last time you cried, you were probably in grade school. That's just the way it is for the male species. One of the challenges a man can face is seeing a child cry, but worse yet, it's seeing a woman cry!

It's not just men, but in reality, no one likes to see a woman cry. When a woman cries, she appears to be weak and so defenseless, that you can't help but want to help her. Women know this and they tend to use it to their advantage if you let them.

The whole idea of a man lacking any form of emotion is totally conditioned from childhood. The fact is, they are human, and under the right circumstances, their emotions will come out. Usually in a fist fight though. In a man's eyes, the only way to stop a woman from crying is to give into her, even if you're saying yes to something you don't want to agree with. Do you honestly believe that she doesn't already know this? Of course she does! She's playing you, and inside she is smiling.

A perfect example would be a man finding out that his wife just got a speeding ticket and it's going to cost him three hundred dollars to pay it off. He sits and stews for a while, his face is red, and his ears have steam coming out of them. Before you know it, he is imagining himself a dragon, and blowing fire from his nostrils. When his wife takes a look at him, she feels totally trapped. She owes him big time, right? Nah, she just turns on the tears, and pierces through his defenses. Who cares if you have to spend the next three weeks working over-time just to make up for the money you lost? She's crying, and he must stop her. He feels responsible for making her cry, and seeing those pretty blue eyes, blood shot and tears streaming down her cheeks totally messes with his mind and his heart strings. He will do anything – as long as she will stop crying! Inside, she continues to smile. It's as though, women are conditioned as little girls to cry and get their own way. This is just one of the many ways that girls and boys are raised as polar opposites. But no worries, opposites, after all, do attract one another. If we were all the same, the world would be pretty darn ordinary.

The Pet Name Game

Pet name, yes, you said it – pet! That's exactly her intentions when she whispers this name you've grown so accustomed to in your ear. For a man, the name is just a name, and quite mechanical. You see these names that you call one another as fondness for one another, or to show your familiarity. But to a woman, it means something totally different.

You know that helpless little dog down the street that barks at you every time you walk by? All he wants from you is a little love and attention, right? With a pet name – you without intention, trade places with that cute little puppy. You might as well have a tail to wag. Disturbing huh?

She knows how to put the creative, seductive twist on that little pet name to make it sound like she's offering you the best night of your life. Again, what's that three letter word that makes men foam at the mouth? S-E-X. She has what you want, and knows how to dress it up in different clothes to make it more appealing. It is her mission to know everything there is to know about the male species, especially YOU! Before you know it, when she says, "honey bear, baby, darling," she makes your head swoon with excitement, and you totally lose all train of thought, thus becoming her pet!

Your attention is totally on her now, as if

you are her puppy and waiting to play fetch or have a delicious meal. She has learned how to put this pet name into a rewarding use for herself, and now she becomes your master. In a relationship there's no room for two masters. In fact, it's probably best that neither of you take up this role, and treat one another with dignity and respect. After all, that's how we build healthy relationships, right? There's nothing wrong with her giving you a pet name, just as long as you know the magical spin she puts on it when she whispers it in your ear. This game can work both ways, trust me.

Chapter 3

The Touching Game

Never underestimate the power of the human touch! Believe it or not, you can transmit so much to the human brain just by touching. Most men think about sex when they touch a woman. Due to this fact, it is basically not appropriate to touch a woman in public – because this constitutes sexual harassment. Women clearly have this advantage over a man. If the woman that you are on a date with reaches across the table and takes a piece of lint off your shoulder, and gives you those stares that are long enough to know that the touch is NOT completely innocent, you are basically at her mercy and she knows it. Don't think for a second that she won't use this to her advantage.

So the next time you find yourself playing footsie under a table with a woman, or she brushes up against you, and hesitates for a moment and your eyes meet – she's is hoping to send shivers through you and make you think she's irresistible to you. More than likely, your brain is going to agree with her at that very moment, and your defenses will be down. If your date has done her homework prior to seeing you, she more than likely knows that a man relates these goose bumps and lapses in speech to being in love. Men are literally in love with being in love. The feelings of newness, and infatuation makes him all mixed up and unlikely to see things through logical eyes. The lack of oxygen to the man's brain will put him on an all time high that can be mistaken for love. She knows this!

A smart woman will take a man on a date to an amusement park, hoping to stir up all kinds of excitement on a roller coaster. Sharing a thrilling ride with someone will make a man suddenly feel a deep connection with that person, and momentarily confuse themselves, relating this confusion with love. A woman armed with this information can be quite manipulative, and she should be viewed not only as a bright shiny star, with luscious kissable lips, but also as someone who knows how to manipulate you to her advantage. This could very well be a turn on to you, and admittedly so, it is a good quality if used for the good. But if you find that she is doing this kind of thing to you too often, and you can not come down from this magical high that she has put you on – it's probably too good to be true. I suggest that you guard yourself, and not give up the control that she so craves from you!

The Comparing Game

No one likes their flaws pointed out to them, and women know this – so they tend to go about it underhandedly. Instead of coming straight out and saying that you aren't doing the things that she thinks you should be doing at home, she will point out all the things that you are doing for other people outside of your home.

So you decided to help the neighbor mow their grass the other day, and you helped your buddy Rick fix his roof the day before that, but at your own home, she's the one keeping

22

everything nice on the home front. When she asks you when you are going to mow the grass, you tell her that your schedule has been so full lately with work and all that you will get to it soon. It's quite common that she will bring it up that you mowed the neighbor's lawn, but can't find the time to mow your own. Or that you chose to spend your only day off fixing Rick's roof instead of being with her. As a result of this, all you can think about is the next time your wife gets together with her friends, she will tell the world about all of your shortcomings. This plays over and over in your head, to the point of driving you insane. You don't want to be the only guy who doesn't help out around the house or have romantic dinner's with his wife.

Then that thought takes you one step

further – into a more dark and twisty place. What if she finds someone else? This is the last thing that you want to happen. Looks like you're mowing the lawn sooner than you thought. She knew you would come around to it. Her tactic worked. Think about it? One simple thing COULD turn into a big conversation with a bunch of chicks sitting in the same room as one another. One of those chicks points out all the great things her man has done for her, making yours feel like crud. This could lead to her thinking that you shouldn't be together, or that you just don't love her enough to make time for her anymore. Then suddenly some "Joe" guy sparks her interest, and she is taken by his empathy and kindness. Soon they start talking, then they start doing more than talking. This more than talking brings you home a sexually transmitted disease that's not curable. Your relationship breaks up and all you can do is think about how you should have made time for her, or mowed your own friggin lawn! Feeling guilty? Of course you are!

Now open your eyes, because all this was just a dream and she hasn't met Joe yet. You go mow the lawn, and she gets what she wanted from you. See how this works? It's not necessarily a bad thing either. Take her comparing game as a *warning sign* that she is still cute, you still want her, and you're not willing to share her with someone else. Don't let her get to far with this game, or you will lose in a big way. In fact, it's probably best that you keep her feeling special so that she doesn't have to play it with you, and you don't have to stress over it and lose sleep, or think about having incurable diseases that make your skin want to crawl.

The Submission Game

The most effective way for a woman to get her man to bend to her wishes is the submission game. Her once strong backbone, now becomes gooey, and she begins to do whatever it is that he asks of her. She knows this is a huge stroke to his ego, and that it will make him feel manly and in control of things. Every man wants a woman who will be obedient and shower him with her affections. He already has a boss at work, and is not looking for another one at home. When a woman becomes submissive to her man, she increases her chances of getting whatever it is that she wants, times ten.

I knew this couple at one time, that were on again, and off again constantly. The girlfriend found her boyfriend's son to be more than a challenge, and quite frankly, she really couldn't stand the kid. He was what she referred to as "the devil's spawn." Each time she would say that, it made me chuckle. I got to hear all of her horror stories of her daily life with this kid, and I totally felt sorry for her. She loved her boyfriend with all of her heart, but knew that if she couldn't form a bond with his son, it just wouldn't work for them. He had physical placement of his son, and therefore he lived in the same house as the two of them.

The one thing that kept them going was the fact that his son would spend summers with his biological mother in a different state. Can you imagine her anxiety to have the house to herself, sharing it only with the man that she loves? So no matter how rough things got for her in that house, she kept her eye on the prize for as long as she could!

The relationship between them became so incredibly predictable. Usually right after school started, the two of them would have some really big fights and she'd move out for a few months. Then they'd get back together again in the Spring. This would be just in time for her to develop a semi – cohesive relationship with the son again before he leaves for the summer, and totally smooth over the relationship with her boyfriend again. She would play the submission game, and bend to his will. Whatever it was that he asked for, she gave to him and his son. She would once again become the mother of the year, as well as the girlfriend of the year. I'm not sure he ever really caught on to it or not, because he would totally propose marriage to her every single summer!

Was he that stupid? Did he not see that no matter how much the two of them loved one another, it was not going to work? Not just with her but anyone! If he couldn't get his kid under control, then he was not going to find happiness anytime soon. Only bits and pieces of it, for short periods of time. After a while, it was as if he believed that her submission to him was love and that he didn't actually have to do anything in return for it. Love to him was something that should just work, and not have to be worked at!

When summer was over, and his son was

home again, his relationship with his girlfriend would suffer, and he would think that she no longer loved him because she suddenly grew a backbone, and stopped being submissive to him. Needless to say, that when she finally left for good, every relationship afterward failed as well. Not only because he now felt that love was a woman being submissive to him, but also because his son made it impossible for any woman to give to him. He was caught up in a delusion that he had grown accustomed to, and expected every woman to follow in the steps of his last one.

Chapter Four

The Avoidance Game

Sometimes a woman feels desperate to get your attention, so she may accomplish this by avoiding you. In your opinion, the two of you are doing fine together, and then suddenly you start to feel that there are miles between you, and you can't do anything right – you can bet that she is playing the avoidance game with you. It's her way of crying out for your attention so that you will show her that you care. She sends you the signals that you are about to lose her. She knows that most people don't try and hold on to anything until they feel they are losing it. You know that saying, "you don't know what you have, until it's gone."

The intelligent woman knows that if she plays this game too long, you will lose interest in her, and may possibly dump her. So she knows when to stop playing the game, and how to still make you feel as if you are in control of everything. A woman this smart, should be feared!

Back to the previous chapter, I told you about this couple who had problems in their relationship due to the son in the home. During those months that they would break up, and she would move out, she knew exactly what she was doing. She knew that by avoiding him, she would get his attention again. At first when she moved out, she would continue regular phone calls to him. Then she would abruptly be too busy to talk to him, and allow for him to imagine her out with her friend having fun, or worse yet – out with another man. This would drive him completely insane!

When she wasn't doing this to him, he was doing this to her until eventually they would have to be together again! Talk about poison – truly this was a toxic relationship. I think that they had both started out with the best of intentions, and sincerely loved one another. But after six years of playing these games with each other – they became addicted to the games themselves instead of the love they once had.

The avoidance game led them back to one another, and she played the obedient, submissive girlfriend over and over and over again! Do yourself a favor. If you see these games being played multiple times, until you are both going in circles and the relationship is not going anywhere new – get out! The only thing it's causing is pain for the both of you, and you only live once. You can not get that time back again. It is NOT love!

The Nagging Game

Men complain that their wives, or girlfriends are always nagging them. It can be quite unbearable to listen to sometimes, and the only way to get her to stop is to consent to her verbal barrage. When you are getting bombarded with constant emails, texts or phone calls, you can feel like your life is no longer your own. This is a very abusive form of controlling someone, even though it might seem innocent at first, and you might actually be flattered by it.

She may indeed keep doing these things until you agree that she can be a pest. Nagging and bombarding you with messages is her way of trying to get what she wants from you, or getting you to act in a certain way toward her. Keep in mind also, that women know how angry men get when they do this – most of them anyway. They just very well might be trying to anger you to strike back. You should sit down with her and see exactly what her motivations are by asking her outright. There just might be the possibility that she has an interest in someone else, and wants you to be the one to break it off with her first! If this is the case, you shouldn't be together in the first place.

Case in point – in the toxic relationship that I have been discussing with you; when she felt the need to get away from his son for a while, she would begin nagging about him in hopes that they would break up for a while, and she could have her freedom once again. Not to mention, a chance to sleep around and make him jealous. We all want what we can't have, right? You bet! Talk about a cat and mouse game – she knew him inside and out, and played him like an old used piano. They used each other for the purpose of driving one another insane.

Sex Games

This is something all women know how to do, and they have all the tools they need at their disposal. Their greatest weapon, being their bodies. If you have a history of losing your self control, all it takes is her revealing a little skin here and there, or kissing you with passion. Men are driven by sex, and for as long as he thinks he will be getting lucky at the end of the day, he will just about do whatever it is that she wants him to do. Another thing that women know, is how to please a man. They know that even if the man doesn't want them as a girlfriend or wife, if she does his bedroom deeds good enough for him, he will always come back! She keeps this in mind, and uses it when it best suits her needs. Usually she will bargain with you, sex for something she wants more than sex.

As for our "toxic couple," she knew she couldn't afford a place to rent on her own, and he owned his own home. For six years, on again, off again, she knew his sexual appetite better than any women around. This was just another one of the games that they played with one another. He got the best sex of his life, and she got to keep him to herself and play housewife minus a payment! All she had to do was put up with his son six months out of the year and keep him from straying.

You might be asking yourself, why not? All is fine if you're having great sex right? For some yes, but the damage psychologically done to the both of them, was way extensive. Neither one of them were worthy of a real loving relationship again. They ruined each other with these games. They both began to mistake the game for love. Not only was she playing the sex game with him, but also with his best friend across the street. But he was so wrapped up in her that he couldn't see it for what it was. He took her back anyway, because she had him convinced that he loved her and that they were meant to be together! Nothing like coming home from work, and checking your driveway for tire tracks that don't belong to you. To him, his paranoia justified his love for her even more.

The Bait Game

So you all know what a "loaded question is," or at least you should by now. It's those questions like, "Do these jeans make me look fat?" "Is this outfit best, or this one?" Women can be pretty creative with such things. Besides feeling desirable to you, she wants you to validate her own opinion. Whatever you do, don't give her a long pause before you answer!

The best way to avoid a melt-down, is to tell her that she looks beautiful in everything she wears, and that you love her no matter what. She might accuse you of just saying that, but it's the only thing you could possibly say that will avoid a confrontation with her, trust me!

Another example of this bait game, again, involves our famous toxic couple. She wanted to get married since she was very young, and never let go of that dream. She also knew that if she was married to him, the house would be half hers and he couldn't make her leave it anymore! So she would bait him with, "We have been together for six years, and you still haven't married me. We are meant to be together, yet you still don't see it." This would leave him pondering for several days, losing much needed sleep. After all, what she said was half truth, and half truths are easy to believe as full truths.

His response to her each time, would be for her to prove that she will stay this time, and if she can prove that to him, then he will marry her.

She'd be the perfect girlfriend for three months,

and again, he'd let her wear the ring. It never

lasted though, because it was just a game.

Chapter Five

The Playing Dumb Game

You know she's intelligent. In fact, if she wasn't you would have never gotten along with her in the first place. You find yourself asking for her help, but since she doesn't want to do what you are asking of her, instead of telling you so, she plays dumb. She doesn't know how to do it, or she doesn't understand what you are asking of her. Basically – she wants you to do it for her. The only way you will get around this situation is to do it yourself, but teach her while you do it. If you do this, she will have no excuse to not know how to do it next time, or to play dumb!

A fine example of this is when your girlfriend needs the tires on her car pumped up.

You tell her at dinner that she can pump up her tires for free at the gas station down the street, or the one over on third street is only fifty cents. She replies with, "OK" Three days later you notice that she still hasn't put air in her tires, and you can hear them coming from a mile away – sounding like a whistle. When you ask her why she hasn't stopped to put air in her tires yet, instead of telling you that she doesn't want to get dirty or whatever, she plays dumb, and tells you she doesn't know how to.

This is also a great excuse for her to use anytime it has to do with the mechanical parts of her car. She forgot how to put oil in the car on her own, or she forgot how to run it through the car wash. More than likely, it's not that she doesn't know how to do these things – she just doesn't want to them herself. It's much easier just to have you do it for her! I also want to bring to your attention that sometimes she may act like she doesn't know how to do something just because she heard from other women that it makes a man feel useful to let him help you, or makes him feel that he is in control. This is usually when she becomes the "damsel in distress." When you take care of her, she feels like you love her.

The Waiting Game

You called her cell phone and left a message. It's been three days and she still hasn't returned your call. Is she still interested in you? The chances are that she is, but here's how to find out. Call her again, and if she takes your calls she is interested, but if she skips it again, she's probably not. I wouldn't attempt calling a third time. The reason why girls can make you wait is that they don't want you to think they are clingy or needy. They also don't want to seem too eager to talk to you. They have probably heard this drives men away, and she doesn't want to drive you away.

Take it from me though. If you leave that second message and she doesn't call you back, she has moved on, and so should you. This may not be the case all the time, but she'd better have a pretty good excuse to keep you on the hook that long. Even so, do not call again. Wait for her to come around. If she wants you, it won't take her too long to get back to you. You can always make time for someone who is important to you, and so can she!

The Hard to Get Game

So she's playing hard to get? This isn't always about her trying to challenge you to chase her. A lot of the time, it is a sure sign that she has been burned badly in her past. She is probably still carrying a load of hurt around on her shoulders, and the only way you are going to convince her that she can give into you is by showing her that you are who you say you are, and that you're not a high risk for her. The best way to counteract this is to let her know that you like her, but don't come on too strong. This will give her the impression that you are clingy and that you are off the market for other dates. She likes you to be a bit of a challenge, just as you like her to be. No one likes, *easy*. If something is too easy, it's usually too good to be true. That goes for both of you.

For those that have been burned in the past and had their hearts smashed into a million pieces, eventually they get really smart and leave the dating life behind for a while. I'm not talking about a few months either. If one is hurt badly enough, it could take a few years before she opens herself up to another man. Just know that good things really are worth waiting for. If you haven't gone out and sewed your wild oats yet, do that before attempting to pass your time as a virgin waiting for this girl! She will be your biggest challenge, and if your heart isn't into it, don't be that last guy who just totally ruins her!

The We Need To Talk Game

The "we need to talk" conversation usually comes up when you're busy playing your play station game, or you just turned on the football game. She wants your attention, and she wants it now, no matter how many of your buddies are in the room. So how do you get through this in the least painful way possible? Simply mute the game and let her talk to you for five minutes. Let her say what she needs to say. Pay attention to her, and act like you care. Then you can un-mute the game and go back to what you were doing. If you have buddies there watching the game with you, it's probably best you go to another room to listen to her though. You don't want your friends mad at you too!

If you tell her you can talk later, prepare yourself for a screaming match. She will yell at you and tell you how much you don't care about her, and later will automatically mean NOW. You won't get a word in edge wise, nor will you be watching or playing that game any time soon! Not to mention, your friends will have a field day teasing you about it later.

The Reverse Psychology Game

What do I mean by the reverse psychology game? This is when she says just the opposite of what she really wants. By doing this she is hoping that you will do what she really wants you to do. A good example of this is when you are both sitting on the couch, and she lets out a deep sigh and proclaims that she has dishes to do. What she really wants is for you to help her do them. But if you don't catch on, it will lead to another argument about you not caring about her, or knowing anything about her etc.

Maybe you really don't want to do the

dishes either, or help do them. Perhaps to please the both of you, you can suggest loading the dishwasher together instead, or you can give her a foot rub or a back massage. Men aren't the only ones who like being soothed! I bet if you do this for her and tell her to just forget about the dishes for tonight, she'd listen to you, and by the time she gets to the dishes tomorrow, she will have long forgot the game she was playing. This will leave her feeling special and not like she's the maid of the house or Cinderella. Sometimes a girl just wants to know that it's OK for her to relax and do nothing.

The Mind Reading Game

She doesn't always want to have to tell you what she wants. She believes that if you can read her mind, then you really do care for her. If you really truly care about her, you will know what she wants. I know this seems unfair, but it is the way it is. So what should you do? Don't play the guessing game with her, because you will just be wasting your time. Instead, come out and ask her what it is that she wants. Tell her that you'd love to make her happy. This will make her feel good that you are listening to her and that you care about making her feel loved.

Women think a lot different than men, and if you tried guessing her thoughts all the time, you would be totally exhausted and lack any ambition to continue on in any romantic escapades with her. This would leave both of you unsatisfied and neither of you wish for that. If there is something that you want to know about her, just ask her. In fact, I will bet my hat that she is dying for you to ask her things in the first place! It makes her feel closer to you and more intimate to share her thoughts with you.

Chapter Six

The Ultimatum Game

You've been dating for three years, and you're still not married. This is the game where she sees just what your made of, and what exactly she means to you. Prepare yourself for the ultimatum. Sometimes they are bluffing. The only way to know is to call them out on it. If they aren't bluffing and your still not ready to tie the knot with her, then this is the time that you should both start considering what your future will be, and whether or not it will involve each other in it. If you have no intentions on marrying her, now is the time to cut your losses.

Maybe you aren't the type of guy who will ever get married. That's fine. You shouldn't change yourself to suit her own beliefs or needs. But you also should not force her to give up her dream to be married and in that committed relationship. Stop denying yourselves the things in life that are important to you. If she wants to marry, let her be free to find that guy that is right for her. You don't want to just give in and marry her, only so you regret it later or resent her for the next twenty years. This will make both of you miserable, and everyone deserves happiness. Believe it or not, there are women out there who don't want to marry either! Go find her instead.

The I'm Pregnant Game

Tread very lightly on this subject. First of all, get it in your mind now that if she is pregnant with your child, you should be man enough to take responsibility. .After all, it really does take two to make babies, and not every woman is desperate enough to lie about being pregnant. Unless she has given you reason to doubt before, give her a little bit of credit that she just might be telling you the truth.

But for the sake of calling this a "game," I can honestly say that there are some women out there who often feel desperate enough to play this game with you. It should be no surprise to you to tell you that most often this card is played when she feels she is losing you!

These women are usually the ones who grew up getting everything they ever wanted from their mommy and daddy. In school they got all the boyfriends, and couldn't eat lunch without a table packed with friends surrounding her. She has always gotten all the attention, and rarely has anyone ever told her no. Girls even followed her to the bathroom! This game would be her last stitch effort to reach out to you and keep you with her. She may feel that you owe her something, and that she was born to be showered with gifts. It actually angers her when you tell her no, and her brain fills with manipulating thoughts. She wants you to pay for her unhappiness. After all it's your fault she's unhappy, because you're the one who wants out of the relationship – not her! Up until this point, nothing else that she has tried has worked, and you still tell her you are leaving.

While laying in bed tossing and turning, she thinks of you with some other girl. This is enough to drive a sane girl insane. If she can't have you no one can. At least in her mind, this is what she is thinking. How can she make you stay? She doesn't want to lose control over the relationship. That's when she gets the brilliant idea that if she is carrying your baby – you won't leave her! After all, what sort of man leaves their woman while she is pregnant? What kind of man wants his child to be raised by another man? How guilty would you feel if you couldn't watch your baby grow up?

This is truly a game of assumptions, really. It's very possible to have a baby with someone and still parent your baby without having a relationship with the baby's mother. People do it all the time. In fact, that's what I am doing – and to be honest, our children are quite happy having two bedrooms, each bedroom, in a different home, in a different part of town. Keep this in mind – just in case she is pregnant. There is no need to be miserable with someone just because you have a child together. A child should add to your life, not take away from it. So don't let your kid grow up thinking that they were resented because their mom is a controlling bitch.

The best way to get quick control of this game is to just call her out on it. If she tells you she wants to have an abortion – ask if you can go with her for comfort. If she isn't pregnant and really getting an abortion, she will probably make up an excuse that keeps you from attending or she might even agree that you can go, then suddenly miscarry the next day.

If she says she wants to keep the baby, tell her that you will support her when the baby comes, but you still are choosing to break up with her. Don't let her use a pregnancy or a fake pregnancy to gain control over you again. Someone who loves you will not do that to you. Also, you should make it very clear to her that you do not want to speak to her about anything unless it has to do with the baby. The chances are that if she really isn't going to have your baby, she will avoid allowing you to see her physically, or she will start coming up with stories to cover the fact that she really isn't pregnant. She may carry on for as long as she can, but it won't take too long before you find out the truth. The truth always has a way of coming out.

The worst thing you can do is to let her know that this game is bothering you. If you don't play along with her, she will lose the game, and eventually quit playing it. Remember, misery loves company – don't let her have the satisfaction. You have one life to live, enjoy it!

The "I Need Some Space" Game

This is one of those games that can be really confusing – but only if you let it! I am going to break it down for you in a short version, and tell you exactly what it means when a woman says she needs some space from you. Nine times out of ten, what she is really saying to you is that she has an interest in someone else, and she needs to see if this someone else is worth dropping you for! Ouch, I know. I am sorry, but there really wasn't much I could say to smooth that over for you. Men aren't the only ones who like to have a backup plan in place when their relationship falls apart. This may not even have been a backup plan – but you can bet that it is in the making as soon as she says those words to you.

Men aren't the only ones who get bored in a relationship either. I think it can be difficult for both men and women to only have sex with one person for the rest of their days. So with that said, this can also be a way for her to express to you that she has the hots for another man, and she wants to try something new for a while. If this is the case, she really doesn't love you – so move on and forget about her. Chances are, that once she has this other guy, she won't look back anyway. The only way she will look back is if you are better in bed than he is, or if the guy doesn't want her for more than one night.

If she is a sneaky kind of girl, but you

know for a fact that she loves you and is still asking you for space – she probably has something in mind that she wants to go do, and she knows that you won't let her if you know about it. Therefore, she tells you she needs some space – so that you can't tell her no, or that she can go do this thing without you knowing about it at all. Feel her out a little bit. Ask questions. Try to find out what is motivating her to get some space from you. People who love one another want to spend time together, not get away from each other. Whether you want to believe it or not, there is an ulterior motive involved. It should be up to you whether or not you play along with this game.

Chapter Seven

The Ex Is Just My Friend Game

There's always the possibility of baggage when you start dating someone new. It takes a lot of maturity to have a girlfriend who is still friends with her ex. At first it may not bother you too much, because she is giving you all the attention and your blinders are on – total infatuation with her. Eventually – these blinders are going to be off, and when you have your first big fight, she calls him to talk to. Whether you want to admit it or not, this is totally going to put doubt in your mind, and squash your ego.

You will probably ask yourself a million times why she is friends with her ex, when you don't talk to any of yours. In fact, you can care less about your own exes. It won't make any sense to you, and it really doesn't to me either, unless they have kids together, and have to stay in some part of each other's lives. I don't know everything, and don't claim to, but I can tell you how best to deal with this game of hers. Become friends with the guy!

Before you close this book, give me a minute to explain. If you are this guy's friend, you can keep a close eye on them both, right? Invite the guy to dinner at your place, where the three of you can sit face to face and you can feel them out. Do they still have chemistry or any sexual energies between them? If they do, you will see it and or feel it between them. Not to mention, the guy will be uncomfortable around you, and might even pass up the opportunity to be your friend in the first place. That would be a dead giveaway, now wouldn't it? If there isn't anything between them anymore, except for their friendship, then you will feel better about things. But if there is still something there, you will call them out on it.

One dead giveaway is if she still can't stop talking about him when you are together. When a woman feels love for someone, she wants to announce it to the world. She will talk about that person every chance she gets. If it ends up that she clearly has feelings for him, you need to sit her down and talk to her about it, not him. Ask her specific questions, tell her what it is that you see between them, and don't let her lie to you. Watch her body language and the words that she uses to answer your questions. If she answers your questions with questions of her own, a red flag should be seen right away.

Don't waste a minute longer with someone who's not in it as much as you are, or with someone who is still hung up on someone else. Sometimes a girl will date someone new and remains friends with the ex, just to see if the ex will get jealous enough to take her back. If this is the case, it's unfair to you and you deserve better.

The Jealousy Game

If you are not exactly dating a girl yet and she talks to you about other guys, or dates that she has coming up, she is more than likely trying to get your attention. She wants to see some sort of jealousy coming from you so that she can see whether or not you are into her. It's her way of testing the waters and seeing what you're not coming out and saying to her. If you are already with a girl and she is talking about other men, or pointing out that oh so hot guy on TV to you – she is basically trying to tell you that you are not at the top of your game, and she wants more from you than what you are initially giving to her. So pay close attention to the types of guys that she is pointing out to you, or the situations that she brings to your attention. It is her way of asking you to give those things to her so that she can be more happy with your relationship.

If you are out in public and you catch her making goo goo eyes with some other guy, don't be afraid to counteract that with a little bit of looking yourself. Don't fly into a huge rage or deprive her of sex for a while, because this will only hurt you! Trust me, girls can hold out on sex for a long time, and you know that's not really what you want to do anyhow. But if she is giving eyes to some other guy, it is because she isn't feeling like she gets enough attention from you, and she wants you to look at her with those eyes again. Most of the time it has nothing to do with liking the guy she is looking at. To her, he is just eye candy. What she really wants is to spark jealousy in you, so that you give her what she wants. So buck up, and give her a night she will remember for a while. It will tame her and bring smiles to both of your faces.

If you suspect she is cheating on you though – she will keep a tight grip on her cell phone, and you won't gain access to it EVER. Keep an eye on this handsome stranger appearing more than once, in many different places that you just happen to be visiting. But like I said, she's is just usually looking for some sort of passion from you. Some girls like it when you bite.

The "I'm Mad" Game

If you are both still young, your girlfriend may play this game on you more often than if you were both older, and more mature. Usually a young woman will play this game of being mad at you, only to see what you will do about it. She wants to see you grovel, and plead with her for forgiveness for whatever you did wrong. She likes the way it feels, and sometimes a young woman may confuse these feelings with love. So if you are not showing her special attention all the time, like you do when you want her forgiveness, she thinks that you don't love her anymore.

Most grown women, are mature enough to not think in such silly ways. But still they can play this game with you, but they mean something totally different when they do. Depending on the woman, it's meaning can vary greatly. If a woman is mad at you, she usually gives you the silent treatment. She wants you to know that you hurt her, and that she needs time to herself right now. The best thing you can do is apologize to her in a way that shows you mean it, and then give her the space that she needs. Let her know the next day that you still know she's upset with you, but don't over do it. A simple kiss or a tender hug is enough to let her know that you are still there when she is ready to talk about it. Whatever you do, don't keep apologizing because that will just annoy her more. If you have any bright ideas to buy her jewelry to make up for your upsetting her – do yourself a favor and save your money! The jewelry will only prolong both of your agony by giving her a daily reminder of the upset.

Another great suggestion is for you to never promise her that you will make changes knowing full well you have no intentions of keeping or fulfilling that promise. Let things blow over naturally. Sit tight, she will come around again, but only when she is ready to forgive you. If your girlfriend is smart and manipulative, she may act as though she is mad at you, just to get you to leave her alone or to use it as an excuse to break up with you. Don't underestimate the power of a woman. She just may not want to be with you anymore. You will know when she can't give you a reason for being upset with you after several days.

The Love Bomb Game

It is very important that you understand this game, if you do not understand anything else in this book. This is the game that can literally take your heart out of your chest, throw it to the ground, and smash it into little tiny pieces that will leave you begging for a heart transplant. No one is lured into a relationship through abuse or criticism. If a woman undermines you on a first date, she will rarely get to the second date with you, unless it's just for sex – and you're using her. The Love Bomb Game is mainly played by a psychopath, and yes there are women out there that have these types of personalities, and they should be totally avoided at all costs. They are only out for themselves, and aim to use you for a specific void that they need filled. Nothing good can come of a relationship with this type of woman.

So what do I mean by a Love Bomb? Once you become a target to a woman such as this, they zero in on you and put on all the charm. They lift you off the ground whispering intoxicating thoughts into your ear, until you feel that you are no longer in control of yourself any longer. It's as if a tornado has come and lifted you into a new dimension of reality. It is very easy to confuse these feelings with love. They treat you like you are the best thing since ice cream, and act like they can not get enough of you. They want to spend every waking minute with you, and it hurts them to be apart from you. They constantly flatter you and give you the best sex you ever had in your life. No one has ever pleased them like you have. No one is as perfect for them as you are. You are so smart and completely understand them. You are the one they have been looking for their whole life. This is the Love Bomb that I am talking about. You are the one true love of their life.

What you truly need to ask yourself is, why is this person whom I just met flattering me so much? Seriously, how many healthy people that you know, go around acting this way? What makes you so special to this person? They act like you hung the moon and stars, yet they barely know anything about you. Could it be that this woman has an ulterior motive? How many times has she told others these same things? How many times has she been in love like this? It's totally not NORMAL!

One of the very first things that your parents taught you while growing up was to not talk to strangers right? Be safe around people you do not know, and that some will offer you all kinds of things to get you in the car with them. These people we call predators, and pedophiles. But now that you are a grown man, why is it that someone can flatter you without you raising a single eyebrow? I suggest that you step away from this bomb for a little while, and get some fresh air. You may need your reasoning skills to save you from a future disaster with this woman.

Psychopaths commonly engage in this

game so that they can sink their claws into a victim. Their declarations of love are only to get you to bond with them, and they do not actually reciprocate the same feelings in return. They want to pump you up with confidence so that they become your new drug of choice. Once you are hooked on them, they can go about their business of getting what they want from you. At this point they begin to play on your weaknesses, and get you focused on anything but them and what they are doing to you. The bond that you have with them can be very dedicated, and totally one sided. This will leave a big gaping hole in your heart the moment you realize that they are sucking the life from you like a leech.

Focus on the signs so that you can avoid

people like this. They are incapable of loving you, and you need to know this. There is nothing that you can do to change them! You can not heal them, or make them better. Run while you still can and avoid this particular game at all costs.

Conclusion

There you have it, 23 mind games that women play with men. Now that you know what makes a woman tick, you might be lucky enough to live a sane life with one! The best advice that I could give to anyone would be to *not settle.* That doesn't mean that you should only look for those that are completely like you and no one else. The truth is, we are all different, and the chances of you finding someone who likes EVERYTHING that you like, is pretty slim.

Stay open minded, and find that someone who doesn't expect you to change everything about yourself to be in a relationship with her. If you do that, you are totally setting yourself up for failure. Find your happy medium. Someone who makes you feel good about yourself, and adds to your life. If she doesn't add to your life, she shouldn't be in it. Same goes for you adding to her life. A relationship can not be one sided. Each partner has to give a certain amount of themselves in a relationship. I have seen way too many relationships fail because one partner gives more or loves more than the other. Life is too short to waste time in these types of scenarios.

It's also best that I tell you not to expect to find a woman who doesn't play games with you. We all play games, admit it! It's just the ones who play them in a way that only benefit themselves, and lack compassion for others around them that you have to be careful of. Never play a game with someone who can play better than you! Just learn the signs given in this book, and counteract them. Enjoy the process and allow yourselves the chance to get to know one another. Knowing these strategies will help you understand women better and learn how to develop lasting relationships with those who are worth your time and respect. Those who play together, stay together!

Other Books Available By Author On Kindle, Audio and Paperback

The 20 Types of Bitches In The World

www.ingramcontent.com/pod-product-compliance
Lightning Source LLC
Chambersburg PA
CBHW070806290526
45795CB00002B/641